Ronald Reagan

A Brief Biography from Beginning to the End

The Biography

History Hub

CONTENTS

Part One: Editor Foreword

"Those who don't know history are doomed to repeat it." — Edmund Burke

More than ever, it is important that we equip ourselves with the power of knowledge to learn from the lessons of mistakes from the past to ensure that we do not fall victim to similar mistakes. It is our aim to provide quality history books for readers to learn important history lessons critical for everyone. And we'd like to make sure you learn the stories faster, and more efficiently.

This is why we are constantly updating our catalog with new releases in History Hub. You can access the catalog of all the new titles here. Thanks for reading, History Hub

Attention: Get Your Free Gift Now

Every <u>purchase</u> now comes with a FREE Bonus Gift

2020 Top 5 Fireside Books of the Year

(New-York Times Bestsellers, USA Today & more)

Chapter One: Ronald Reagan

Did You Know?

Ronald Reagan enjoyed eating jellybeans. As per the Ronald Reagan Presidential Library, his preferred flavor was licorice. Reagan began eating jam beans in 1967 as he was attempting to stop his habit of pipe-smoking.

†††

In a small community of Tampico, Illinois, Ronald Wilson Reagan was born to John "Jack" Reagan and Nelle Wilson Reagan on February 6, 1911. Similarly, as other different young men experiencing childhood in the Midwest after the turn of the century, Reagan was of primarily Irish descent. His father was an Irish-American shoe salesman, and his mother was of Scottish-Irish descent. Reagan used the name "Dutch" throughout his childhood since he did not like his given name. According to some, his father had said that Ronald Reagan appeared as a "fat little Dutchman" when he was born. Reagan had just one sibling, an older brother named Neil.

All through Reagan's earlier years, his family moved a couple of times through Illinois, living in Tampico, Chicago, Galesburg, Monmouth, and Dixon, where the family settled when Ronald Reagan was nine years of age. Due to their frequent moves to different places, Reagan did not make many lasting friendships. Instead, he sought his family for company, as did the other three Reagans. Thus, the four turned into a closely-knit unit. The family lived in an apartment that needed indoor pipes and running water situated along the small community's central street. The family was so close and acquainted that when the siblings were in secondary school, they began calling their parents by their first names. Before moving to Dixon, Ronald Reagan was additionally a somewhat independent kid. He delighted in playing without anyone else with his tin soldiers. He was particularly pleased to read books about natural history. In his memoirs, Reagan recalled that when he was a child, he had read his preferred book on wolves so often that years after he could recite the whole book word for word. He enhanced these books with a little assortment of mounted butterflies that had been given to him.

Ronald Reagan also recalled that Dixon, Illinois, where the family finally settled, was the ideal spot for him to spend his adolescence. During that time, Dixon was a settlement of around 10,000 individuals with a definite network and friendship feeling. Everybody in the community knew one another and helped each other amid hardships. Reagan had finally made friends in Dixon and spent numerous days tromping through the forested areas around the town, swimming, and fishing in the Rock River and catching muskrats. For instance, when Reagan was eleven years of age, he propelled a little illegal rocket into the Dixon bridge's side. Reagan, therefore, earned himself a trip to the police headquarters and a costly fine. He likewise got himself into several fistfights with different boys.

Ronald Reagan was not wholly a rascal. Actually, by the age of eleven, he had gotten genuinely sincere. He had decided for himself that he wanted to be sanctified in the Disciple of Christ. His mother was also a Disciple of Christ, yet had never compelled her children to become devotees themselves. Her mother accepted that every individual ought to have the opportunity to decide their faith since her other half was Catholic. Luckily, the differences in religion in the family never caused any trouble. However, it taught Reagan that not every person had similar beliefs. Her mother did, in any case, impart in her children her sense of respectability. She solidly trusted in aiding those less fortunate than herself and had a strong belief in prohibition. Ironically, her husband was a drunkard, yet she never reprimanded him for what she accepted to be his "sickness." Reagan decided to turn into a disciple because a character in one of his preferred books, The Printer of Udell's, was a devout Christian. Ronald Reagan stayed a religious man for his entire life.

Both Ronald Reagan's parents did not receive formal education in their lives; they only had gone to grammar school for just a couple of years. His father, Jack, had gone to the American School of Proctipedics and earned his shoe sales diploma. All through Ronald Reagan's youth and pre-adulthood, his father longed for owning his retail shoe establishment. Generally, the Reagan family was not wealthy, barely able to make a decent living. Then again, Reagan later composed that what his parents needed proper training, they made up for in "street smarts." They urged their children to buckle down in school and improve something of themselves too. One time, they discovered racial discrimination appalling. They urged Neil and Ronald to bring their Jewish and African-American companions home with them regardless of whether doing so would cost them their popularity.

Fireside Question 1

†††

Ronald Reagan used the nickname "Dutch" during his childhood because he did not like his name. Some people said that his father told them that Ronald Reagan appeared as a "fat little Dutchman" when he was born. Why do you think Reagan did not like his given name?

_____

_____

_____

_____

_____

_____

_____

_____

_____

_____

Fireside Question 2

†††

During Reagan's childhood, they frequently moved through Illinois, living in Tampico, Chicago, Galesburg, Monmouth, and Dixon. Because of this, Reagan never had a long-lasting friendship until they finally settled in Dixon. What could be the reason for his family's frequent moving through the state?

_____

_____

_____

_____

_____

_____

_____

_____

_____

_____

_____

Fireside Question 3

††††

Because of their regular move to different places, the family found a company in each other. They became so close to the point that when the siblings reached high school, they began calling their parents by their first names. Do you think this is a sign of disrespect even if they are close? Why do you say so?

_____

_____

_____

_____

_____

_____

_____

_____

_____

_____

Fireside Question 4

Reagan became a rascal in his late childhood and got even involved in several fistfights. One day, he decided to be baptized as a Disciple of Christ, which is his mother's religion. What could happen if Reagan still had not baptized himself as a Disciple of Christ? Will he still be the same Reagan who always got involved in several fights?

Fireside Question 5

†††

Reagan became a rascal in his late childhood and got even involved in several fistfights. One day, he decided to be baptized as a Disciple of Christ, which is his mother's religion. What could happen if Reagan still had not baptized himself as a Disciple of Christ? Will he still be the same Reagan who always got involved in several fights?

Chapter Two: Ronald Reagan

Did You Know?

During his adolescent years, Ronald Reagan was successful as an actor and football player at Eureka College. Yet, his most significant job was as a lifeguard at a neighborhood park in Illinois. Reagan spared an expected 77 lives in his summers doing this job.

†††

Regardless of his parents' advice to do well in school, Reagan involved himself more in sports than he did in whatever else at Dixon's North Side High School. He especially adored football and was regarded for his spirit and hard-working attitude. However, Reagan was not the best player. He additionally delighted in acting and started to lead in a few churches and school plays. Through his acting skills, Dixon's people realized he was not the quiet and introverted kid numerous individuals thought he was. Reagan became one of the most well-liked and popular young men in his school, and by his senior year, he had been chosen as the president of the student body.

Ronald Reagan entered Disciples of Christ Eureka College in 1928 in Eureka, Illinois. In secondary school, he was not the best student since he invested most of his energy in participating in school activities. He also became a popular student figure when he drove a strike to fight the school's choice to lay off instructors as the Depression drew closer. During his years at Eureka, Reagan was a football and track sports player and became the captain of the swimming team. He was a member of the basketball cheering squad, a yearbook editorial manager, and was chosen as the Booster Club President and Student Body President. Reagan likewise won a few prestigious acting awards. He studied economics and sociology and finished at Eureka College in 1932.

In the spring of 1937, while in Southern California to cover the training season of the Chicago Cubs, Ronald Reagan did a screen test for the Warner Brothers film studio. The studio signed him to an agreement, and that same year he made his movie debut as a radio journalist in "Love is On the Air." Throughout the following thirty years, he showed up in more than 50 motion pictures. Among his most famous roles was Notre Dame football star George Gipp in the 1940 historical film "Knute Rockne All American." In the movie, Reagan's favorite line–which he is still remembered for, was "Win one for the Gipper." Another remarkable role was in 1942 in "Kings Row," in which Reagan depicted a victim from a tragic accident who awakens to find his legs have been cut off and shouts out, "Where's the rest of me?" which Reagan utilized as the title of his 1965 autobiography.

In his adolescent years, Ronald Reagan was a Democratic Party member and campaigned for Democratic representatives. However, his perspectives became more conservative after some time, and in the mid-1960s, he formally turned into a Republican. In 1964, Reagan ventured into the public political spotlight when he gave a welcomed televised discourse for

Republican presidential candidate Barry Goldwater, a popular conservative. In his first race in politics, Reagan won against the Democratic candidate Edmund "Pat" Brown Sr. by nearly 1 million votes for California's governorship. Reagan was reappointed to a second term in 1970.

After making fruitless offers for the Republican presidential selection in 1968 and 1976, Reagan got his party's nod in 1980. In that year's political race, he and running mate George H.W. Bush went head to head against President Jimmy Carter and Vice President Walter Mondale. Reagan won the election by a margin of 489-49 and got almost 51 percent of the vote. At age 69, he was the oldest individual to become the United States president. On March 30, 1981, two months after his inauguration, Ronald Reagan survived an assassination attempt by John Hinckley Jr., who is said to be with a history of mental issues, outside a hotel in Washington, D.C. The bullet pierced one of Reagan's lungs and barely missed his heart. Reagan, known for his good humor, later told his significant other, "Honey, I forgot to duck." A couple of weeks after the shooting, Reagan went back to work.

Ronald Reagan and his significant other came back to Los Angeles, California, after leaving the White House in January 1989. In November 1994, Reagan told in a handwritten letter to the American individuals that he had been diagnosed with Alzheimer's disease. Almost ten years later, on June 5, 2004, he died at his home in Los Angeles at 93 years old, making him the country's longest-lived president. Gerald Ford, however, surpassed him for this title in 2006. Reagan was given a state memorial service in Washington, D.C., and later buried in his presidential library grounds.

Fireside Question 6

†††

Ronald Reagan did not follow his parents' advice to achieve good grades in school. Instead, he participated in numerous school activities and sports. Why do you think Reagan chose to be active in sports and other school activities rather than good grades?

_____

_____

_____

_____

_____

_____

_____

_____

_____

_____

Fireside Question 7

†††

People were surprised after knowing that Reagan joined in various school activities and even started acting. They thought Reagan was an introverted and quiet kid. Do you believe Reagan is introverted or quiet? If yes, how did he overcome this personality to try new things in his school?

_____

_____

_____

_____

_____

_____

_____

_____

_____

_____

Fireside Question 8

†††

Reagan became a famous student figure because of leading a strike to fight the school's choice to lay off instructors as the Depression drew closer. Do you think this was the stepping stone of Reagan to enter public office? Did people believe Reagan might become an excellent public servant someday?

Fireside Question 9

†††

While studying at Eureka College, Reagan was a football player, a yearbook editor, and a basketball cheering squad member. In the end, he pursued acting, which he signed a contract with Warner Bros. What do you think Ronald Reagan saw in acting that he did not see in his other activities?

_____

_____

_____

_____

_____

_____

_____

_____

_____

_____

Fireside Question 10

During his adolescent years, Reagan was a Democratic party member and even campaigned for the party's representatives. However, his views changed and became more conservative, which led him to join the Republican party. What could be the reason for Reagan's change of perspective?

Chapter Three: Ronald Reagan

Did You Know?

Ronald Reagan was the first president elected to have been divorced. He got married to an actress, Jane Wyman, during the 1940s and was separated in 1948. He wedded Nancy Davis, an actress as well, in 1952.

†††

Ronald Reagan started his career as an actor when he did a screen test for the Warner Brothers movie studio in the spring of 1937. This studio gave him his first role as a radio news reporter at a film entitled "Love is On the Air." Three decades later, he starred in more than fifty films. Reagan's well-known roles included George Gipp, a Notre Dame football star in the 1940 biographical movie "Knute Rockne All American." Another prominent role was a portrayal of a victim in an accident who woke up discovering his legs have been amputated in 1942's movie "Kings Row," wherein his famous line "Where's the rest of me?" was used as the title of his autobiography in 1965.

In 1940, Ronald Reagan got married to an actress named Jane Wyman, with whom he had a little girl named Maureen and an adopted child, Michael. The couple separated in 1948 and later on, he got married to another actress, Nancy Davis, in 1952. The pair had two youngsters, Patricia and Ronald.

During World War II, Reagan was excluded from combat duty because of low eye vision. Instead, he invested his time in the Army, making training films.

From 1947 to 1952, and from 1959 to 1960, he was the president of the Screen Actors Guild (SAG). During that time, he affirmed before the House Un-American Activities Committee (HUAC). From 1954 to 1962, he facilitated the weekly TV drama series "The General Electric Theater." In this series, he visited the United States as a public relations representative for General Electric. He gave business talks in which he revolted against excessive government control and inefficient spending, focal subjects of his future political career.

Ronald Reagan was part of the Democratic Party during his teenage years and campaigned for Democratic representatives. Still, his perspectives developed into a more conservative after some time, and in the mid-1960s, he officially turned into a Republican. In 1964, Reagan ventured into the public political spotlight when he gave a generally welcomed broadcast discourse for Republican presidential candidate Barry Goldwater, a well-known conservative. In his first race for public office, he was elected as the governor of California against the incumbent Democrat Edmund "Pat" Brown Sr. He was reappointed in 1970. In 1980, he ran for the presidency. He won with his running mate, George H.W. Bush, against President Jimmy Carter and Vice President Walter Mondale. Ronald Reagan was sworn into office on January 20, 1981. In his address, Reagan broadly said of America's then-disturbed economy, "In this current emergency, the government is not the answer for our issues; the government is the issue." In 1981, Reagan left a mark on the world by selecting Sandra Day O'Connor as the first woman to the United States Supreme Court.

President Ronald Reagan actualized approaches to diminish the national government's venture into Americans' everyday lives and wallets, including tax reductions expected to spike development (known as Reaganomics). He also supported increments in military spending, decreases in specific social projects, and deregulates business. By 1983, the country's economy had begun to recoup and enter a time of success that would stretch out through the remainder of Reagan's administration. Critics kept up that his policies prompted budget deficits and a more significant debt; some likewise held that his economic projects supported the rich.

In November 1984, Ronald Reagan was reappointed in a landslide. He won against Walter Mondale and his running mate Geraldine Ferraro, the first female vice-presidential candidate from a major United States political party. Reagan, who declared it was "morning again in America," got 49 of 50 states in the election and got 525 out of 538 constituent votes, the most significant number won by an American presidential candidate. During his subsequent term, Reagan produced a diplomatic relationship with Mikhail Gorbachev, who became a pioneer of the Soviet Union in 1985. In 1987, the Americans and Soviets signed a special arrangement to eliminate nuclear missiles. In the same year, Reagan talked at Germany's Berlin Wall, an image of communism, and Gorbachev to destroy it. After 29 months, Gorbachev permitted the individuals of Berlin to destroy the wall. When Reagan left the White House, he returned to Germany in September 1900, weeks before

Germany was formally reunified, and took a few symbolic swings with a mallet at a remaining piece of the wall.

Fireside Question 11

†††

One of the famous films starring Ronald Reagan was "Kings Row." He even used his favorite line in the movie as the title for his 1965 autobiography. Why do you think Reagan chose this line to be the title of his autobiography?

Fireside Question 12

†††

Years later, in his acting career, he facilitated the TV drama series "The General Electric Theater." This TV series became an opportunity for Reagan to give business talks against excessive government control and inefficient spending. When Reagan became the president, do you think he addressed extreme government control and weak spending? Elaborate on your answer.

Fireside Question 13

†††

Ronald Reagan won in his presidential race against President Jimmy Carter. In his first term, he took a significant step by appointing Sandra Day O'Connor, the first woman to become part of the United States Supreme Court. What could be the implication of Reagan's actions?

_____

_____

_____

_____

_____

_____

_____

_____

_____

_____

Fireside Question 14

†††

When Reagan ran for the presidency for his second term, he won by a landslide against Walter Mondale. During his first term, he implemented Reaganomics, an economical approach to diminish the national government's venture into Americans' everyday lives and wallets, including tax reductions. Do you think Reaganomics played a big part in Reagan's victory for his second term as the United States president? Why do you say so?

Fireside Question 15

Reagan had an agreement with Gorbachev regarding the tearing down of the Berlin Wall. He was very eager for this agreement because even after his term ended, he went to Berlin to make a few symbolic swings of his hammer to destroy the wall's remaining piece. What could be the significance of tearing down the Berlin Wall to the people of Berlin?

Chapter Four: Ronald Reagan

Did You Know?

Ronald Reagan hated brussels sprouts. Nancy Reagan said he was certainly
not a fussy eater since he went on the public speaking circuit for a
considerable length of time, however, he additionally hated tomatoes.

†††

Becoming successful in both political and acting careers was never easy for
Ronald Reagan. His struggle started during his earlier years. He never had
any long-lasting friendships because of frequent moves made by the Reagan
family throughout Illinois. Having a friend at that age was vital to enjoying
his childhood. Luckily, the family became his company, which made the
bond of the family stronger.

Another challenge struck the Reagan family when the Depression
happened. For Reagan to pay for his education and help his family during the
Depression, he worked various secondary school and college jobs. His least
liked job was cooking burgers at Eureka College. He also washed tables in
the ladies' residence and worked as a lifeguard for seven consecutive
summers at Lowell Park on the Rock River in Dixon. He worked for twelve
hours every day for seven days per week. During those summers, Reagan

spared 77 swimmers from drowning in the river. Ten years later, as President, Reagan considered his job as a lifeguard as one of his best accomplishments.

After finishing college in 1932, Reagan faced two setbacks that changed his life. First, Margaret Cleaver, the girl he had dated for a long time since secondary school and school, left him for another man. The two became engaged when they finished college and decided to get married when she returned from her teaching job and a tour to Europe. However, before the year ended, she returned the engagement ring to him via mail. She sent a note clarifying she had gotten engaged to another man in Europe. Second, during the peak of the Depression, occupations were rare, and Montgomery Ward was not just known for its lucrative positions at $12.50 every week, but also its stability. Unfortunately, the boss decided to hire a fresh athletic secondary school graduate. Reagan had to search somewhere else for money.

Decades later, Reagan joined the Republican Party in 1962. After four years, Reagan announced his aim to run for the governorship of California. At first, Reagan had a horrible campaign style; numerous voters associated him with Barry Goldwater. Reagan himself experienced difficulty talking in front of several liberal Californians. Once, he even stomped out of a theater while addressing the National Negro Republican Assembly when somebody in the crowd yelled that he was racist. As the campaign progressed, Reagan turned out to be significantly more sure about his capacities. He promoted his image as an ordinary American who needed lower taxes, harmony, fewer crimes, government assistance change, and decreased government spending. He attacked his competitor, incumbent Pat Brown, for neglecting to suppress student violence on California college campuses and for overspending. Pat

Brown ignored the actor-turned-politician and even traveled in Europe during the campaign. That November, Reagan won the elections, taking 53 of California's 58 regions and gaining over a million more votes than Brown.

It is usual for a government official to face challenges during his term. During his period, Reagan needed to give up many of his campaign promises when faced with political reality. His first crisis came when the legislature unexpectedly had a tremendous budget shortfall. To save money, Reagan cut a modest amount of spending in every division of the administration. Even though this sounded reasonable and worked in specific divisions, it is still not sufficient. For instance, due to spending cuts, vast numbers of the state mental institutions needed to deliver unstable patients to save money. Reagan solidified government spending and even sold the state jet. At last, Governor Reagan repealed his promise to reduce government expenditures when he expanded the state income tax to cash.

After two terms as the governor of the State of California, he ran for the presidency. He lost at the first attempt but finally won in his second attempt. On March 30, 1981, two months after the inauguration, Reagan was shot underneath his arm by a man outside the Washington Hilton Hotel. The assassin was John Hinckley, a mentally disturbed man from Colorado. Surprisingly, Hinckley did not shoot Reagan for political reasons or individual ones. He attempted to kill Reagan to impress the actress Jodie Foster, who had starred in the well-known film Taxi Driver. Reagan was rushed to the hospital. He managed how to get through rapidly and returned to the Oval Office much more popular than ever.

During the 1970s to 1980s, the nation was in a deep recession. Energy costs topped, inflation was high, and numerous Americans were unemployed. Therefore, Americans needed change. President Reagan entered the presidency with clear objectives to roll out improvements. Tired of many years of liberal social policy, Reagan needed to lessen the size and function of government in the United States. His agenda focused on curtailing government expenditures, adjusting the budget, withdrawing support from government assistance programs, and restoring some state governments' powers. For Reagan, if the United States could achieve these objectives, the government could simultaneously spare billions of dollars and stimulate the economy.

When Ronald Reagan left the White House, his retirement was not that happy. In February 1990, Reagan was summoned to testify in an investigation of the Iran-Contra scandal. Reagan's journals from the period being referred to were additionally called. Reagan testified in July 1992 and asserted he was unable to recall that anything about the scandal. Reagan claimed he was unable to remember the previous executive of his Joint Chiefs of Staff. Reagan was disposed of as a potential witness. Years later, Ronald Reagan was diagnosed with Alzheimer's Disease. Reagan was not lying when he said that he could not remember much about the Iran-Contra scandal.

Fireside Question 16

†††

Several difficulties faced by Reagan during childhood and adolescent stage were mentioned in this text. What do you think was the most difficult for Reagan? Explain your answer.

_____

_____

_____

_____

_____

_____

_____

_____

_____

_____

Fireside Question 17

†††

Ronald Reagan worked different jobs to help his family and to pay for his education during the Depression. How do you think Reagan managed his time studying, working, and participating in school activities? Was there any moment of your life that you faced this kind of struggle? If yes, how did you manage it?

_____

_____

_____

_____

_____

_____

_____

_____

_____

_____

_____

Fireside Question 18

According to the text, Ronald Reagan faced two setbacks that changed his life. These setbacks include being left by his girlfriend and his struggle to find a job during the Depression. Do you agree that these two changed Reagan's lives? Why do you say so?

_____

_____

_____

_____

_____

_____

_____

_____

_____

_____

Fireside Question 19

†††

Ronald Reagan ran for public office for the first time as the governor of California. At first, he had difficulties delivering a speech in front of the public, but he later managed it. How do you think Reagan managed his difficulty in public speaking?

_____

_____

_____

_____

_____

_____

_____

_____

_____

_____

Fireside Question 20

†††

Problems that happened during Reagan's presidency were mentioned in this text. What do you think was the most challenging problem to solve for Reagan? Elaborate on your answer.

_____

_____

_____

_____

_____

_____

_____

_____

_____

_____

_____

Chapter Five: Ronald Reagan

Did You Know?

Ronald Reagan lost hearing partially in one ear when he was harmed on a film set in the 1930s after a weapon was shot close to his ear. Decades later, he kept in touch with Michael Jackson offering his help after Jackson was burned filming a TV ad.

†††

Ronald Reagan became a roughneck during his early adolescent stage. However, he decided to become devout through baptism into the Disciple of Christ, which is his mother's religion. His mother did not pressure her sons to become disciples because she believed that each person should have the choice to determine his or her faith. One of the reasons why Reagan chose to become a disciple because a character in one of his favorite books, The Printer of Udell's, was a Christian. Reagan remained a religious man throughout his life.

Although he had no intention of becoming part of the military, Reagan joined the Army Reserve. His reason was for the opportunity to ride horses. His friends in Iowa introduced him to horseback riding, and he grew to love it. Reagan found out that if he joined the reserves at Fort Des Moines, he could ride horses any time for free. He signed up for the military training program. Reagan became a reserve officer in the Fort Des Moines Fourteenth Cavalry Regiment. He never expected that he would report for active duty.

In 1937, because of his friends at the radio station signed by the movie studios, Ronald Reagan decided that he could become a professional actor. That is why he convinced his boss at the WHO Des Moines radio station to cover the Chicago Cubs' spring training at Los Angeles. His ulterior motive was to see if he could make it in the motion picture industry.

When Reagan was in Hollywood in 1937, numerous actors convinced him to join the new Screen Actors Guild (SAG). However, Reagan did not have any desire to join the organization. After hearing his colleague's stories about actors who were forced out of the industry, he decided to join. Later on, he became part of the SAG board of directors for several years and became the president in 1946. As the SAG leader, Reagan visited Hollywood and the nation giving talks about the film business and the protection needed by small actors working their way to the top. He also made addresses against what he accepted to be a nascent fascist movement in America. Generally, Reagan's crowds would cheer and applaud during his talks. Yet, they would frequently become curbed when he mentioned the wrongs of Communism.

Ronald Reagan was originally a Democrat and decided to join the Republican Party in 1962. Several factors contributed to Reagan's conversion, which includes, a) his hate towards Communists and Soviet sympathizers; b) the majority of the influential members of the Reagan family were Republicans and c) he disliked the liberal politicians in California and blamed them for social unrest and budget deficits in 1950 to 1960.

Reagan's famous contribution during his presidency, the Reaganomics, was based on the works of economist Arthur Laffer. Laffer argued that reducing government expenditures for the businesses and wealthier quarter of American residents would support spending and put more cash into the economy overall. The money would then inevitably "trickle-down" or discover its way into the middle and less fortunate Americans' classes, improving everybody off. Laffer's hypothesis was referred to as supply-side economic theory or, all the more informally, Reaganomics because Reagan pioneered the strategies.

Fireside Question 21

†††

Several people and things that played a significant role in Reagan's life were mentioned in this text. Who or what could have played a most significant influence on Reagan? Why do you say so?

_____

_____

_____

_____

_____

_____

_____

_____

_____

_____

_____

Fireside Question 22

†††

One of the reasons Reagan decided to be baptized as a Disciple of Christ was the character in his favorite book, a Christian. If Reagan did not read this book, do you think his mother is enough to decide to join in the Disciple of Christ? Explain your answer.

_____

_____

_____

_____

_____

_____

_____

_____

_____

_____

Fireside Question 23

†††

At first, Reagan did not want to join the SAG but later became part of the board of directors. He also became the president years later and gave speeches about protecting small actors and his hate towards communism. What could be the source of Reagan's hatred towards the communists?

_____

_____

_____

_____

_____

_____

_____

_____

_____

_____

Fireside Question 24

†††

Ronald Reagan was originally a Democrat but decided to convert to the Republican Party in 1962. Several factors were mentioned in his decision for changing parties. Among these factors, what do you think was the biggest reason why Reagan joined the Republican Party?

_____

_____

_____

_____

_____

_____

_____

_____

_____

_____

Fireside Question 25

†††

Reaganomics was primarily based on Arthur Laffer's supply-side economic theory. Do you think the said economic strategy deserves to be called Reaganomics, although this was based mainly on Laffer's concept? Elaborate on your answer.

_____

_____

_____

_____

_____

_____

_____

_____

_____

_____

Chapter Six: Conclusion

Did You Know?

Ronald Reagan began life as a Democrat and upheld the New Deal endeavors of President Franklin D. Roosevelt. Reagan turned into a Republican in 1962, however, he became more conservative during the 1950s as he visited as a General Electric spokesman.

††††

Ronald Reagan's most significant accomplishments were mostly during his presidency. Some of his legacies include appointing the first woman to the United States Supreme Court, the Reaganomics, conquering the Cold War, and the Strategic Defense Initiative. All of these left a significant impact on Americans.

On August 19, 1981, President Ronald Reagan fulfilled his 1980 campaign promise by choosing Sandra Day O'Connor as the first woman to get a position at the Supreme Court. During this time, the fifty-one-year-old O'Connor was an appointed judge in the Arizona Court of Appeals and had a recognized profession. She also served as Arizona's Assistant Attorney General in the Arizona Senate. She was the first female state majority leader in the nation. She was appointed judge of the Maricopa County Superior Court.

During Reagan's term, a deep recession happened in the United States in the 1970s to 1980s. Americans wanted change, as energy prices are at a peak, the unemployment rate was high, and inflation was also increased. To solve the crisis, Ronald Reagan implemented Reaganomics, one of his most notable contributions to society. In this type of economic policy, Reagan diminished domestic spending and increased military spending, making a net deficiency all through his two terms. The top marginal tax rate on individual salary was cut to 28% from 70%, and the corporate tax rate was decreased from 48% to 34%. Reagan reduced the economic regulation that started under President Jimmy Carter and wiped out price controls on oil and gaseous petrol, long-distance telephone utilities, and satellite TV. In his subsequent foreign currencies. When Reagan's second term was almost to an end, tax revenues from the United States government expanded to $909 billion in 1988 from $517 billion in 1980. Inflation was decreased to 4%, and the unemployment rate fell beneath 6%. Although financial experts and government officials keep arguing over Reaganomics' impacts, it introduced one of the most extended and most grounded times of success in American history. Somewhere between 1982 and 2000, the Dow Jones Industrial Average (DJIA) grew about 14-fold, and the economy included 40 million new jobs.

Another Reagan's accomplishment during his presidency was conquering the Cold War. President Reagan faced down worldwide threats of communism with a strength that many express that this led to the Soviet Union's collapse. A key component of Reagan's triumph was the help of anti-communist powers in Afghanistan, Nicaragua, Angola, and Cambodia. The "Reagan Doctrine" was the most practical of all the cold war doctrines. It cost the United States less than a billion dollars per year while constraining the Soviets to spend $8 billion yearly to avoid its effect. Likewise, it was one of the most politically successful doctrines in Cold War history. It brought about a Soviet pullout from Afghanistan, the appointment of a democratic government in Nicaragua, and the expulsion of 40,000 Cuban soldiers from Angola and United Nations-monitored elections.

The Strategic Defense Initiative was another legacy of President Reagan. Reagan pioneered national defense with a program that unified military strategies and innovation to counteract atomic war threats. A New Vision of the GOP: Reagan, known as the Great Communicator, utilized his charm to put a new face. Strategic Defense Initiative, also called Star Wars, proposed a defensive system against potential nuclear attacks. President Ronald Reagan first proposed it in a televised address on March 23, 1983.

Fireside Question 26

Some of Reagan's notable accomplishments were mentioned in the above text, including Reaganomics, appointing the first woman to the Supreme Court, conquering the Cold War, and the Strategic Defense Initiative. Among these contributions, which of these left a most significant impact on the Americans? Why do you say so?

_____

_____

_____

_____

_____

_____

_____

_____

_____

_____

Fireside Question 27

†††

During the 1980 campaign, Reagan promised to appoint the first woman to the United States Supreme Court and did not break that promise when he won the presidency. What could be the implication in Reagan's goals in his term? Does he want gender equality, or he did this to promote his image to the Americans?

Fireside Question 28

†††

Reaganomics became one of the most successful economic strategies in American history. Yet, some people and government officials were criticizing Reagan because of its impacts. Do you think Reaganomics benefited more Americans or not? Explain your answer.

_____

_____

_____

_____

_____

_____

_____

_____

_____

_____

Fireside Question 29

President Reagan spent much of his time solving the problem with the Soviet Union. What is the Soviet Union? Does it pose a risk to the countries during that time?

_____

_____

_____

_____

_____

_____

_____

_____

_____

_____

Fireside Question 30

†††

In the Strategic Defense Initiative, Reagan was known as the Great Communicator. Why do you think Reagan was given this title? Does utilizing his charm have something to do with becoming a great communicator?

_____

_____

_____

_____

_____

_____

_____

_____

_____

_____

Attention: Get Your Free Gift Now

Every <u>purchase</u> now comes with a FREE Bonus Gift

2020 Top 5 Fireside Books of the Year

(New-York Times Bestsellers, USA Today & more)

<u>Get it now here:</u>

<u>Scan QR Code to Download Free Gift</u>

q ``

Printed in Great Britain
by Amazon

77802033R00034